KT-144-046 ◢

Nelson MANDELA

LIZ GOGERLY

www.heinemann.co.uk/library

Visit our website to find out more information about **Heinemann Library** books.

To order:
- ☎ Phone 44 (0) 1865 888066
- 🖹 Send a fax to 44 (0) 1865 314091
- 🖥 Visit the Heinemann Bookshop at www.heinemann.co.uk/library to browse our catalogue and order online.

First published in Great Britain by Heinemann Library, Halley Court, Jordan Hill, Oxford OX2 8EJ, part of Harcourt Education.

Heinemann is a registered trademark of Harcourt Education Ltd.

Produced for Heinemann by Discovery Books Ltd
Editorial: Gill Humphrey, Nicole Irving, Andrew Solway and Jennifer Tubbs
Design: Ian Winton
Illustrations: Stefan Chabluk
Picture research: Rachel Tisdale
Production: Séverine Ribierre

Originated by Dot Gradations
Printed and bound in China by South China Printing Company

ISBN 0 431 13883 4
07 06 05 04 03
10 9 8 7 6 5 4 3 2 1

British Library Cataloguing in Publication Data
Gogerly, Liz
  Nelson Mandela. – (Leading lives)
  968'.06'092

A full catalogue record for this book is available from the British Library.

Acknowledgements
The publishers would like to thank the following for permission to reproduce photographs: Corbis: pp. **4, 9, 13, 18, 39, 41, 42, 47, 48, 49, 51, 54**; Hulton Archive: p. **38**; UWC RIM Mayibuye Archives: pp. **10, 15, 21, 23, 25, 30, 32, 34, 36**; Popperfoto: pp. **5, 12, 17, 20, 26, 27, 44, 52, 53**; Topham: p. **33**.

Cover photograph of Nelson Mandela reproduced with permission of Corbis.

Every effort has been made to contact copyright holders of any material reproduced in this book. Any omissions will be rectified in subsequent printings if notice is given to the publishers.

Disclaimer
All the Internet addresses (URLs) given in this book were valid at the time of going to press. However, due to the dynamic nature of the Internet, some addresses may have changed, or sites may have ceased to exist since publication. While the author and publishers regret any inconvenience this may cause readers, no responsibility for any such changes can be accepted by either the author or the publishers.

Contents

Any words appearing in the text in bold, **like this**, are explained in the Glossary.

The people's choice

On 27 April 1994 voting began in South Africa's first all-race **democratic** election. Until then the right to vote had been denied to millions of black people. Only white people could vote, even though the majority of people living in South Africa were black. Therefore the eyes of the world were watching as this historic event took place. In rural areas some people had walked for three days to take their place in the long queues leading to the polling booths. Many were barefoot, without food or water, but they waited patiently as the hot sun beat down. All across the country similar queues gathered throughout the five days of voting.

◀ *Black South Africans joining long queues in the Transkei to vote in the first all-race democratic elections in 1994.*

Mandela's first vote

At Ohlange High School in Natal a greying 75-year-old black man was about to cast the first vote of his life. Over 300 journalists had gathered to record this special moment. Nelson Mandela was famous throughout the world and everybody knew where he would place his mark on the **ballot** sheet. Mandela would be voting for the African National **Congress** (ANC), an organization of which he was already president. Many millions of South Africans would also be voting for the ANC and pinning their hopes on this man

▶ *A smiling Nelson Mandela casts the first vote of his life in the 1994 elections in South Africa. Mandela's party, the ANC, won 62.6 per cent of the vote.*

who had spent over 27 years in prison because of his belief in equal rights and his opposition to the rule of his country by a white minority. At the end of the 1980s South Africa had a population of over 40 million people, but only 5 million of these were white. White people controlled the government of South Africa and benefited most from the country's wealth.

Nelson Mandela had played a crucial role in gaining equality for blacks, even though he had been captive on Robben Island, one of the harshest and most remote prisons in the world. This day was like the end of a journey, a long struggle that Mandela has famously called, 'a long walk to freedom'. His vision of South Africa as a 'rainbow nation', where everyone had the right to vote whatever their skin colour, was about to be realized.

A better life for all

Nelson Mandela had been freed from Robben Island in February 1990. During the previous decades demonstrations and violent protests claimed many lives as blacks fought against the harsh and unjust laws of the white government. The country needed a political figure who could unify South Africa and bring peace. Mandela talked of South Africans putting the past behind them and re-building their country. ANC banners claimed that Mandela was 'The People's Choice' and that the ANC would bring 'A Better Life for All'. Black and white people placed their faith in Mandela, and on 10 May 1994 he became the first black president of South Africa.

The country boy

Nelson Mandela was born on 18 July 1918 in Mvezo, a small village in the Transkei region of South Africa. As he was a **Xhosa** (ZOE-sah) his father gave him a Xhosa name – Rolihlahla, which translated means 'troublemaker'. Mandela's father, Gadla Henry Mphakanyiswa, was a descendant of the Thembu royal family, part of the Xhosa people, and chief of Mvezo. Under British **colonial** rule, the Thembus no longer held any real power but Mandela's father was still treated with respect by the black community. As was tradition with the Xhosa people, Mandela's father had taken four wives. Mandela was the son of his third wife, Nosekeni Fanny, and he lived with her in a group of three beehive-shaped homes with mud walls in the village of Qunu. They lived on the crops they grew and the animals they raised on a few neighbouring fields. Mandela spent most of his time with his mother and his sisters, Mabel and Leabie, but also enjoyed playing with his many half-brothers and sisters who lived nearby.

Nature's playground

Like the other children in his village Mandela enjoyed the simple pleasures of the surrounding countryside. He would run around barefooted on the green fields and swim in the clear streams and rivers nearby. Games included hide-and-seek or fighting with sticks. Toys were the little animals and birds that he had modelled from clay. Life was happy and carefree, even when at the age of five he became a herd boy. Now Mandela was responsible for looking after his family's cattle, goats and sheep, and sometimes he slept out under the stars sharing a blanket with the other herd boys. Mandela watched and learned how to provide more food for his family. He was taught how to hunt birds, and where to find wild honey and to collect fruits and berries. His childhood may well have been simple but Mandela described those times as 'some of the happiest years of my boyhood'.

Lessons in life

When Mandela was seven he became the first child in his family to go to school. Wearing his father's trousers, cut down to fit, he attended the local **Methodist** schoolhouse. It was on his first day that his teacher Miss Mdingane gave him the English name Nelson. This was a custom among African teachers at this time. A few years later, in 1927, his life changed again when his father died from a lung disease. Now aged nine Mandela was taken to live at the 'Great Palace' of his father's friend Chief Jongintaba Dalindyebo. The chief was the regent of the Thembu people, which meant that he ruled in place of his elderly father, and Mandela's father had asked him to take in and educate his son if he should die.

▼ *This map of South Africa shows some of the important places in Nelson Mandela's life.*

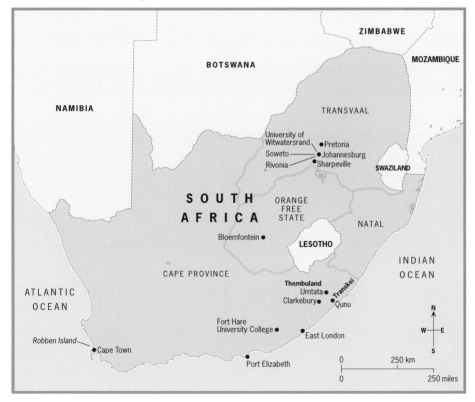

The 'Great Palace' was nothing more than a cluster of simple buildings and homes, and the regent drove an old Ford motor car, but to the young Mandela this was a massive step upwards. The regent and his wife, who was called 'No England', treated Mandela as if he were their own son. They sent him to a new Methodist school next to the palace, and expected him to help farm their land. Mandela described his new home as a 'magical kingdom' where he could enjoy riding horses and dancing and singing along to traditional Xhosa songs. By listening to the stories of the local leaders he also learned more about the history of his people, the Xhosa, as well as other African tribes. He heard stories about African heroes who had fought against the white man. For the first time he became aware of what had happened to his country. The stories made him 'feel angry and cheated, as though I had already been robbed of my own birthright'.

South Africa

In the centuries before Nelson Mandela was born the black peoples of South Africa suffered greatly as a result of British and Dutch settlement of the region. Illnesses, like smallpox, that arrived along with the settlers, killed many blacks. Others were simply hunted down and murdered. From early times whites believed themselves superior to blacks, whom they treated like children. In fact the Boers (descendants of the original Dutch settlers) believed they had a god-given right to use the blacks as slaves.

▲ *This photograph, taken sometime in the 1940s, shows a white woman training black South Africans to be domestic servants. They would have addressed her as 'Madam' and called her husband 'Master' at all times.*

To locate the places mentioned, see the map of South Africa on page 7.

When Nelson Mandela was a child South Africa was made up of four colonies that had once been ruled by the British. Two of these colonies, Transvaal and the Orange Free State, had belonged to the Boers (these people later became known as **Afrikaners**) but were conquered by the British at the end of the 19th and the beginning of the 20th centuries. Many Africans fought on the side of the British in these wars, but when the battles were over the Africans were refused the right to vote in elections. In the following years more laws were passed that restricted non-whites to menial jobs (jobs that require very little skill – like working as servants). Black South Africans would continue to be treated as second-class citizens for much of the 20th century.

An English education

Mandela did well at school and when he was sixteen the regent sent him to Clarkebury, a good Methodist school run by British **missionaries**. Two years later he was sent to Healdtown, another Methodist school. Mandela enjoyed both schools although they taught mostly Methodism, British history and geography. 'As a teenager in the countryside,' Mandela wrote, 'I knew about London and Glasgow as much as I knew about Cape Town and Johannesburg.' Years later Mandela praised the missionaries who had taught him, and pointed out that many black children under **apartheid** did not receive as good an education as the one he had.

▲ At just 17 years old Nelson Mandela looks smart and confident. This is one of the earliest known photographs of him.

College life

In 1938 Mandela went to Fort Hare, a small university for black students. Fort Hare took only the best black students and Mandela felt proud to attend. By now he was a tall, well-mannered and smartly-dressed young man. He studied law, administration, politics and English, though he was better at sports such as boxing or cross-country running. Some of the other students at Fort Hare were active in politics. One of these was a bright young man called Oliver Tambo. Years later Tambo would become Mandela's great friend and work partner, but at Fort Hare the two young men hardly knew one another. At this time Mandela had no real interest in politics and was considering becoming a **civil servant**.

FOR DETAILS ON KEY PEOPLE OF MANDELA'S TIME, SEE PAGES **58-9**.

A rebellious streak

Until then Mandela had been obedient and hard-working, but in his second year at Fort Hare he discovered his rebellious streak. White students at other universities had better food than the students at Fort Hare. In protest many of the black students **boycotted** the elections for student representatives, and those that were elected, including Mandela, handed in their resignations saying they supported the demands of the majority of the students.

Even though he was threatened with **expulsion**, Mandela stood firm. He was expelled a few days later and returned to the Great Palace to face the regent. His guardian was furious and demanded that Mandela return to college and make his apologies. Mandela did neither of these things, but within weeks he had something new to worry about. The regent did not have long to live and he had arranged marriages for his son, Justice, and for Mandela. Mandela wasn't attracted to the woman the regent had chosen for him and believed that she was already in love with Justice. He believed that the only solution was to run away. Justice had decided to run away too and they plotted their getaway together. The opportunity to flee came in April 1941 while the Regent was away from the palace. With one suitcase between them they escaped to Johannesburg, the biggest city in South Africa.

The city of gold

In 1941 Johannesburg was just 55 years old and known as the 'city of gold'. It was an exciting city founded on the wealth of the gold and diamonds that were mined there. Skyscrapers, modern buildings, grand hotels, even a cathedral, graced the city centre. While the white Europeans who owned and managed the mines lived in prosperous suburbs, the poorer black Africans who worked the mines were squeezed into **townships** where there was no electricity or running water. Mandela and Justice joined the thousands of other black people who had come to Johannesburg in search of jobs and prosperity. Mandela was lucky enough to meet a black estate agent and businessman called Walter Sisulu who would have a profound effect upon his future.

FOR DETAILS ON KEY PEOPLE OF MANDELA'S TIME, SEE PAGES 58-9.

The trainee lawyer

When Walter Sisulu met Nelson Mandela for the first time he saw beyond the fresh-faced country boy. 'I marked him at once as a man with great qualities, who was destined to play an important part,' he later claimed. Mandela admired Sisulu

▼ An aerial photograph of Johannesburg taken around 1947, a few years after Mandela made his home there. The white spoil heaps from the mines can be seen in the background.

too, and told him that he wanted to become a lawyer. Sisulu introduced him to a Jewish lawyer, Lazar Sidelsky, who was impressed enough to hire him as a trainee lawyer and give him one of his old suits. Mandela never forgot this kindness and described Sidelsky as 'the first white man who treated me as a human being.'

Life in a township

Mandela found lodgings in the black township of Alexandra. In the **ramshackle**, overcrowded housing lived Zulus, Swazis and Sothos, as well as **Xhosas**. For the first time Mandela experienced the diversity and spirit of African culture. He saw people struggling to survive on low wages, yet still able to laugh. Although he was poor, and often had to walk the nineteen kilometres (twelve miles) to work rather than pay the bus fare, he felt he had discovered a new richness to life.

Further education

Mandela saw the regent only one more time, when the old man paid him a visit at the end of 1941. By then the regent had forgiven him, and Mandela had made a new life for himself in Johannesburg. In 1942 the regent died and soon afterwards Mandela completed his BA degree through a **correspondence course**.

▶ The end of a long shift for workers at one of Johannesburg's gold mines in 1948. Conditions were often dangerous and these men would have gone down as far as 1200 metres to look for gold.

Once Mandela had believed that a BA degree would be his passport to the future, but now he wanted a law degree from the University of Witwatersrand. 'Wits' was one of the few South African universities that admitted both white and black students. Mandela studied law there on a part-time basis for six years. Long working hours made it difficult to study, and at university he was often made uncomfortable by the white students who sometimes called him a 'kaffir', an extremely insulting term for black people. Mandela was disappointed that he never managed to get his law degree at Wits, but he met people from different races and backgrounds. He made friends with **Afrikaners**, Indians and Jews, and he had lively political debates about **communism** and **civil rights**. Inspired by new ideas and beliefs, Mandela felt himself becoming more politically aware.

Founding of the ANC

Black African leaders first met in Bloemfontein, central South Africa, in 1912 and formed the South African Native National Convention (now known as the African National Congress, or ANC). To begin with, the aim of the organization was to pressure the government to change the racial laws. But by the 1940s the ANC was calling for 'one man, one vote,' the abolition of the **pass laws**, **trade union** rights and better health and education services for black people. At their first meeting they sang the song 'Nkosi Sikelel iAfrika'(God bless Africa), which became the anthem for the ANC party and is now the national anthem of South Africa.

Political awakening

By 1943 Mandela had moved to the township of Orlando, part of present-day Soweto (SOuth WEstern TOwnship). That year he also joined a march of 10,000 blacks protesting against a bus company's decision to raise bus fares. This was his first real contact with the political group the African National **Congress** (ANC). Mandela had moved to Orlando to be closer to his friend Walter Sisulu. The Sisulus' house was a hotbed of political activity and Mandela met inspiring people like Anton Lembede. This proud young Zulu had a law degree and spoke **eloquently** and passionately about civil rights. Lembede believed that Africa belonged to Africans, not white Europeans, and thought that mass action was the only way to demonstrate against **white supremacy** – the belief held by many whites that they were superior to people of other races. In April, Lembede launched the ANC Youth League with Nelson Mandela, Walter Sisulu, and Oliver Tambo on the committee. Mandela's fight for **democracy** and **liberation** for black South Africans had begun.

Setting up home

It was at Sisulu's home that Mandela met a pretty young nurse called Evelyn Mase. They were married in 1944 and a year later they had their first child, a son they named Thembi. The young family moved into one of the hundreds of tiny houses built in Orlando. There was no electricity and they only had an outside toilet 'but it was my first true home of my own,' wrote Mandela, 'and I was mightily proud'. Mandela continued to work as a legal clerk and in the rare moments he was at home he helped his wife with shopping, cooking and looking after their baby, which was very unusual for a man at that time.

▶ *Nelson Mandela with his first wife Evelyn Mase in about 1944. Their wedding was a quiet ceremony as they could not afford a proper wedding feast.*

Separate lives

By 1947 Mandela had worked as a legal clerk for three years, but to practise as an **attorney** he needed his law degree. That spring he gave up his position at Sidelsky's law office and took out a loan so he could continue to study at Wits on a full-time basis. Soon afterwards Evelyn gave birth to another child, a daughter they named Makaziwe. With no real income Mandela found it a struggle to feed his young family. Always weak and sickly, Makaziwe died from a mystery illness when she was nine months old. In the same year Anton Lembede, the leader of the ANC Youth League, also died suddenly. The new president, Peter Mda, was a less fiery man than his **predecessor**, but he was still determined to see an end to **white supremacy**.

Apartheid

In 1948 the white government in South Africa was about to take a harder line on black South Africans. In the general election, in which only white people could vote, the National Party, headed by the Afrikaner Dr. Daniel Malan, had taken power. In his election campaign Malan had proposed a new policy of '**apartheid**,' a term which means 'separateness'. He described a new system whereby blacks and whites would be separated or **segregated** in all spheres of life. It would become the law that people of different colour would live in separate areas and use different facilities. Although South Africa was already a deeply divided society the introduction of apartheid would make white supremacy legally binding. Mandela was 'stunned and dismayed' when he heard about the victory of the National Party, '…we knew that our land would henceforth be a place of tension and strife,' he later wrote.

Whites only

Within weeks of Malan's government taking office, signs proclaiming 'Whites Only' appeared on train carriages, but this

Living under apartheid

In 1952 the government introduced new **pass laws** and from then on non-whites had to carry a pass with them at all times. Their movements were restricted to special areas and if non-whites were caught in a white residential area without a special permit they could be arrested. In 1953 the Bantu Education Act completely separated schooling for whites and blacks. In history lessons non-whites were supposed to be taught that they were inferior, but often teachers taught them the real history of South Africa.

was only a beginning. In the next five years laws were passed that turned South Africa into an apartheid state. People were classified as white, Asian, coloured (mixed-race) or native (black). Each race lived in separate areas, went to separate schools or hospitals, even used separate beaches, cafes and cinemas. It even became the law that people of different races could no

▲ Life under apartheid meant separate park benches for blacks and whites, as well as separate doctors' waiting rooms and entrances to buildings.

longer marry. To make matters worse, non-whites were always provided with the worst homes and poor public services. Mandela was scornful of a system that decided where one could live and work, 'on such absurd distinctions as the curl of one's hair or the size of one's lips'.

Fighting back

In 1947 Mandela became a leader of the ANC Youth League, and in 1949 he became a prominent member of the ANC. In the past the ANC had kept its activities within the law, but in the face of apartheid it began advocating **mass demonstrations** such as **boycotts**, **strikes** and **stay-at-homes**.

The inspiration behind this new tactic was Mahatma Gandhi, who in 1946 had fought against British **colonial** rule in India by staging peaceful protests. At this time it was against the law for black South Africans to strike, and as ANC leaders, Mandela, Tambo and Sisulu had to be prepared to go to prison for their beliefs. Mandela's wife, Evelyn, was not political and in the early days of their marriage had tolerated Mandela's role in the Youth League. Now politics was taking him away from home more often. Evelyn turned more to religion and the couple began to drift apart. With politics came fame, and soon Mandela was a well-known figure in Orlando. At 1.9 metres (six feet two inches) tall he was a massive presence. His smart suits, his large smile and his slightly aloof and regal air added to his charm.

▲ *Mahatma Gandhi (1869–1948), pictured here on the right with Nehru, India's first prime minister, practised as a lawyer in South Africa for twenty years. When he returned to India he led a peaceful protest movement against British rule. The success of his methods influenced the way the ANC organized their own protests.*

Laying down the law

In 1950 Mandela was elected National President of the
Youth League. That same year he witnessed the police turn
on a peaceful demonstration in Orlando calling for freedom
of speech, in which eighteen blacks were killed. 'That day
was a turning point in my life,' Mandela later claimed. He
realized that the fight against **apartheid** would be difficult
and possibly bloody, but he took heart because it showed
that Africans were prepared to stand up for their rights. In
1950 the ANC also joined forces with the South African
Indian **Congress** (SAIC) and on 26 June staged a National
Day of Protest. It was the first country-wide political
protest organized by the ANC. Many black workers stayed
at home that day, shops closed and a demonstration of 5000
people took place. That same day Mandela's second son,
Makgatho Lewanika was born. Though Mandela was there
for his birth, he had spent so little time at home that his
first son, Thembi, had recently asked Evelyn, 'Where does
Daddy live?'

The Defiance Campaign

Throughout 1951 the ANC and SAIC made plans for the
Campaign for the Defiance of Unjust Laws (the Defiance
Campaign for short). This campaign would involve **mass
demonstrations** and deliberate **violation** of race laws. By
wilfully ignoring 'White Only' signs and using European
facilities such as toilets, the plan was for thousands of
people to be arrested and imprisoned. The ANC hoped the
campaign would show the government the strength of
opposition to apartheid. As these plans took shape,
Mandela's career as a lawyer progressed. By then he had
worked for three different white law practices and had
finally become a qualified **attorney**. Now his sights were
set on opening his own practice in partnership with Oliver

▲ *South Africans of all races banded together to protest against unjust apartheid laws during the Defiance Campaign. These men have just been released from prison for breaking the law.*

TO LOCATE THE PLACES MENTIONED, SEE THE MAP OF SOUTH AFRICA ON PAGE 7.

Tambo.

On 26 June 1952 the Defiance Campaign was launched, and in the following five months 8600 volunteers went to jail. In July 1952 Mandela was also arrested, though he was charged with being a **communist** (people who opposed the government were often described as 'communists'). For blacks involved in the Defiance Campaign, going to prison soon became a badge of honour. In October, however, the campaign began to dwindle when riots broke out in Port Elizabeth and East London. Though the riots were nothing to do with the Defiance Campaign, the government increased the sentences of anybody defying apartheid laws. By the end of 1952 the Defiance Campaign had ended, but membership of the ANC had increased from 7000 to about 100,000 members.

Mandela and Tambo

In August 1952 Mandela and Tambo's law firm opened for business. It was the first black African law firm in South Africa. They were official attorneys to the ANC, but 'Mandela and Tambo' helped ordinary people too, particularly those involved in wrangles over confiscated land (**evictions** of blacks from their homes were common under the apartheid system), or people arrested for violating apartheid laws. During the Defiance Campaign the **Law Society** tried to have the practice closed down. Mandela also felt the squeeze

on his political activities as he was **banned** by the South
African government from making public speeches, taking part
in group activities, or leaving Johannesburg. Tense times
followed as policemen kept watch over his activities. Mandela
described his ban as 'a kind of walking imprisonment' because
if he were caught ignoring the ban he would be put in jail. By
now Mandela was in his early thirties with a life divided
between politics and
work, but because he was
being watched his political
life became more secret.

▶ *Nelson Mandela (right)
and Dr. Yusuf Dadoo (left)
leave court during the
Defiance Campaign. Dadoo
was the president of the SAIC
(South African Indian
Congress) and was one of the
organizers of the Defiance
Campaign.*

The M Plan

At the end of 1952 Mandela became one of the four deputy
presidents of the ANC. In order for the ANC to continue its
work effectively it had to be an **underground** movement so
Mandela devised the M Plan (M stands for Mandela). The M
Plan detailed how the ANC would be divided into
underground groups. Public meetings were banned so
meetings and lectures were held in houses, or other private
places. In June 1953 Mandela's ban expired for a short while
and he spoke in front of a crowd at a protest rally in
Sophiatown in Johannesburg. The crowd was angry and for
the first time Mandela told them to prepare for violent
struggle. This sudden outburst was because he felt frustrated,
but he soon realized that he had spoken rashly.

New alliances

Mandela's impulsive battle cry earned him criticism from some members of the ANC who believed that the South African authorities would get tougher if they felt threatened by violent **revolution**. Though Mandela was told he should preach peaceful resistance, in his heart he believed that 'non-violence was not the answer'. In September 1953 Mandela's movements were restricted once more. This time he was not only **banned** from attending meetings or leaving Johannesburg, but he was also required to resign from the ANC. Though the ban was imposed for two years, Mandela still worked secretly for the ANC.

The Congress of the People

In 1954 the ANC planned a **Congress** of the People to be held the following year. This would be a mass event attended by the ANC and representatives from other anti-**apartheid** groups such as the South African Indian Congress (SAIC) and the South African Coloured People's Organization. In the run-up to the event they distributed millions of leaflets throughout the country asking people what laws they would make and how they would govern South Africa. The people's responses to these questions were drawn up and became the Freedom **Charter**. Mandela did not draft the charter but was consulted about its content: 'It was humbling to see how the suggestions of ordinary people were often far ahead of those of the leaders,' he later said.

On 25 and 26 June 1955 thousands of people gathered for the congress at Kliptown, near Soweto in Johannesburg. Mandela was under a banning order at the time and so he disguised himself and watched from a distance as the Freedom Charter was read out paragraph by paragraph. This important charter would become the ANC's blueprint for freedom for the next four decades. On the second day of the congress armed police stormed the stage and accused the attendants of **treason**. As thousands of people were rounded up by the police, Mandela made his escape. 'I knew that this **raid** signalled a harsh new turn on the part of the government,' he later wrote. In many ways the Congress of the People had been a success. All those organizations that supported the charter became a stronger union that would from then on be known as the Congress Alliance.

Freedom Charter

'We, the people of South Africa, declare for all our country and the world to know:

That South Africa belongs to all who live in it, black and white, and that no government can justly claim authority unless it is based on the will of the people;...

That our country will never be prosperous or free until all our people live in brotherhood, enjoying equal rights and opportunities.'

(Excerpts from the Congress of the People's Freedom Charter, 1955)

▶ Young children attempt to hand out leaflets for the Freedom Charter. Although some white people helped to compile the charter, most whites refused to take part.

Family ties

By September 1955 Mandela's ban had lapsed so he made a trip home to the Transkei to visit his mother. Her life was still as simple and humble as he remembered his own childhood had been. Feeling guilty he questioned his role in the freedom struggle. 'I wonder – not for the first time – whether one was ever justified in neglecting the welfare of one's own family in order to fight for the welfare of others,' he wrote. Even though politics had taken over much of his life Mandela still found some time for his family back in Orlando. In 1953 the Mandelas had another baby girl who they named after their first daughter, Makaziwe ('Maki'). Sometimes in the evenings he took his son Thembi to boxing training. His political activities, however, took up so much of his time that he had little of it left to spend with his family.

The Treason Trial

Since the Congress of the People rumours of mass arrests had been circulating and in December 1956 Mandela's young family watched as he was arrested and taken away. Along with 155 others, including Oliver Tambo and Walter Sisulu, he was accused of high treason for his part in a plot to overthrow the government. His involvement in drawing up the Freedom Charter was used as evidence against him. For two weeks the accused were held in a Johannesburg prison called 'the Fort', then they were released on **bail** and allowed to go home until the trial. The 'Treason Trial', as it would become known, was a long drawn-out event that lasted until 1961. Throughout this time the police monitored Mandela's activities and he had to report to the police each week. Loud knocks on the door in the middle of the night and spells in prison became a regular part of his life.

TREASON TRIAL

The ACCUSED

DECEMBER 1956

▲ *A montage of those accused in the Treason Trial, including Nelson Mandela (circled, third row, eight from the right).*

An empty home

When Mandela was released on bail for Christmas 1956 he returned to an empty home. For a long time Evelyn had been upset about his involvement in politics and she told him to make a choice between family life and his commitment to politics. When he couldn't make this choice she left him, taking the children with her. Mandela noticed how their marriage break-up affected their children. Makaziwe didn't know whether to smile or frown at him, while Thembi had started to wear his father's clothes. 'They gave him some kind of attachment to his too often distant father,' he wrote. Soon afterwards Mandela met a young woman called Winnie Nomzamo Madikizela and fell deeply and passionately in love.

The freedom fighter

Mandela married Winnie in June 1958, just a year after their first meeting and his divorce from Evelyn. At the wedding Winnie's father warned his daughter that she was marrying a

▲ *A broadly smiling Nelson Mandela poses with his new bride, Winnie Madikizela Mandela, in 1958. He was attracted to her spirit, her courage and her wilfulness.*

man who was already wedded to the struggle against **apartheid**. **Raids** by the police on their Orlando home became more frequent as police searched for **incriminating** evidence against Mandela. Another problem was that Mandela and Tambo's law practice was beginning to fall apart. Increasingly the Mandelas would have to rely upon Winnie's salary as a social worker. Winnie accepted these changes to her life and soon became politically active herself by joining the ANC Women's League. In October 1958 she was arrested and imprisoned for two weeks when she took part in a demonstration against **pass laws**, which restricted the movement of blacks by forcing them to carry **passbooks**. These stormy times were, however, lightened by the arrival of their first daughter Zenani ('Zeni') in February 1959.

FOR DETAILS ON KEY PEOPLE OF MANDELA'S TIME, SEE PAGES 58-9.

Fury in Sharpeville

In 1960 a wave of optimism swept the African continent as some African countries celebrated their independence (or move towards independence) from European rule. In South Africa these feelings soon disappeared when events turned violent in Sharpeville, a **township** 35 miles south of Johannesburg. On 22 March another anti-apartheid group, the Pan Africanist **Congress** (PAC) had organized a demonstration against pass laws in which 10,000 unarmed protestors had gathered around the police station in Sharpeville. The police had turned on the crowd with guns and shot at the demonstrators even as they turned to run. Sixty-nine people had been killed and more than four hundred others had been injured. Horrific photographs of the massacre made front-page news across the world. The country was in crisis and the ANC responded with **strikes**, burning of pass books, a day of mourning and more marches. Even though he had no part in the Sharpeville demonstration, Mandela was arrested and thrown in prison again. Oliver Tambo fled to Dar-es-Salaam in Tanganyika (now Tanzania) to set up ANC offices abroad. A **revolution** in South Africa seemed imminent. To prevent their loss of power the government announced a **state of emergency** and declared that the ANC and other anti-apartheid groups were illegal.

◀ *Armed police move amongst the bodies of the victims of the Sharpeville massacre in March 1960. Photographs like this alerted the world to the mounting tensions within South Africa.*

Mandela remained in prison for the next five months until the state of emergency was lifted. By now the law practice had closed down but he continued to pick up legal work where he could. That December Winnie gave birth to their second daughter, Zindziswa ('Zindzi'). Throughout this period Mandela was often back in court defending himself in the **Treason** Trial. He now stood out as a leader as he publicly argued the case for the ANC. In March 1961 he was finally found not guilty and for the first time in years he wasn't living under a government ban.

The Black Pimpernel

In South Africa in 1961, Nelson Mandela became a new national hero. He was named the 'Black Pimpernel' after the Scarlet Pimpernel, a hero in a book who saves many innocent people from death during the French Revolution. Fearing he would be arrested or put under a ban Mandela spent the next seventeen months of his life as a **fugitive**. While he was undercover Mandela and the ANC organized a mass **stay-at-home**, a demonstration in which people refused to go to work between the 29 and the 31 May 1961. On the first day 10,000 people went on strike, but on the second day a police clamp-down forced the protestors to call off their demonstration. In May 1961 South Africa left the British Commonwealth to become a **republic**. Black people were more scared than ever and believed that harsher apartheid laws would follow. In June, Mandela called a secret meeting of the ANC National Executive and proposed that violence should be used in their war against apartheid.

Spear of the Nation

Mandela finally convinced the ANC to form *Umkhonto we Sizwe* (Spear of the Nation) or the MK for short, a **terrorist** wing of the ANC. Mandela had never been trained as a soldier; he had never even used a gun against a **guerrilla** enemy, and now he had the daunting task of **recruiting** volunteers and training an army. He travelled throughout South Africa, often disguised as a chauffeur or gardener, recruiting people for the army. During this time he took great risks by staying in the houses of white people living in white areas, who supported the ANC's aims. If he were discovered there would be trouble not only for himself but also for his white supporters. Mandela also experimented with explosives and tried them out at night. In October he moved to a more permanent hideout, at Liliesleaf Farm in Rivonia, a suburb of Johannesburg.

It was decided that MK would begin its campaign of violence with **sabotage**. They hoped that attacks on power plants, telephone lines, transport links and army bases would affect the economy of the country and bring about the collapse of the government. If this did not happen they were prepared to try other terrorist acts. Occasionally Winnie and the girls would make secret visits. These special times together helped them all to forget the dangers that Mandela was facing.

Travels abroad

In January 1962 Mandela made another dangerous decision. Even though he had promised the government he wouldn't leave South Africa he agreed to represent the ANC at a conference of African nations and freedom organizations being held in Ethiopia. It would be his first visit abroad, and it would also be an opportunity to meet leaders of other independent African countries and perhaps raise political and economic support for MK.

'For the first time in my life, I was a free man ... Everywhere I went in Tanganyika my skin colour was automatically accepted rather than instantly **reviled**.'

(Mandela's comments on how differently he was treated in countries ruled by black Africans. From *Long Walk to Freedom*, 1994.)

▲ *Together in Europe in 1962: Nelson Mandela shares a joke with his life-long friend and partner in business and politics, Oliver Tambo.*

Next he travelled to Ghana where he met Oliver Tambo for the first time in over two years. Mandela was impressed with Tambo's success at establishing ANC offices in Tanganyika, Ghana, Egypt and the UK. They travelled to Ethiopia together and Mandela spoke at the conference. Mandela went on to visit Egypt, Nigeria and the UK before returning to Ethiopia where he spent two months in military training. In July the South African government passed a Sabotage Bill that meant anybody found to be plotting against the government could be given the death penalty. Desperate to pin something on Mandela, the government had, in his absence, raided his home.

On trial

In July 1962 Mandela arrived back in South Africa and the following month he was arrested and charged with incitement to strike and leaving the country without a passport. Over the next months Winnie watched as her husband conducted his own defence in court. Once more he was being held in prison and on one occasion when he was allowed to meet his wife they talked about how she would support their family. Winnie was working, some of Mandela's clients still owed him money, and with the help of friends they hoped she would be able to manage. On 7 November Mandela was given a five-year prison sentence with hard labour. As he was driven away Mandela took great heart from the crowds of supporters around the court who sang 'Nkosi Sikelel' iAfrika' (God bless Africa). At first he was sent to Pretoria prison, but after six months he was transferred to one of the most forbidding prisons in the world – Robben Island. This **maximum security prison** is located eleven kilometres (seven miles) off the coast of Cape Town, South Africa. Even though Mandela was totally cut off from the outside world his reputation as the hero of the freedom struggle grew.

TO LOCATE THE PLACES MENTIONED, SEE THE MAP OF SOUTH AFRICA ON PAGE 7.

Trial speech

'I have done my duty to my people and to South Africa. I have no doubt that posterity [future generations] will pronounce that I was innocent and that the criminals that should have been brought before this court are the members of the government.'

(Mandela's speech before his sentence, November 1962. From Long Walk to Freedom, 1994)

A life sentence

In July 1963 police **raided** the farm at Rivonia and seized information about MK. They found documents in Nelson Mandela's handwriting. It was all they needed to accuse him of **treason**. At Robben Island Mandela was told of this dreadful news. That night a prison guard banged on his cell door and told him that he need not worry about sleeping saying, 'You are going to sleep for a long, long time.' The guard meant that he thought Mandela was going to be executed.

The Rivonia Trial

Mandela was transferred to Pretoria prison for the duration of the Rivonia Trial which opened in October 1963. Among the seven others on trial was Mandela's close friend, Walter Sisulu. When Mandela appeared in court he looked thin and gaunt, but when he turned to the spectators he gave them one of his broad smiles – there was hope yet. The Rivonia Trial would become one of the most famous trials in South African history, and it was during this trial that Mandela emerged as a powerful leader of his people.

◀ *Known as the 'Rivonia Eight', these men were sentenced to life imprisonment in 1964. Top row: Nelson Mandela, Walter Sisulu, Govan Mbeki (father of Thabo Mbeki, the current president of South Africa) and Raymond Mhlaba. Bottom row: Elias Motsoaledi, Andrew Mlangeni, Ahmed Kathrada and Dennis Goldberg.*

► The pain shows in the faces of Mandela's wife, Winnie, and his mother, Nosekeni Fanny, as they leave Pretoria Supreme Court where Mandela has just been sentenced to life imprisonment in July 1964.

Once again he chose to defend himself so he could explain his political ideas. His concluding speech lasted four hours. On 12 June 1964 'the Rivonia Eight' were found guilty of **sabotage** and sentenced to life imprisonment. There was a gasp of relief in the courtroom when the sentence was announced – they had escaped the death penalty. As he was led away Mandela tried to catch Winnie's eye, but in the commotion he couldn't see her. On the drive from the court Mandela heard the rousing words of 'Nkosi Sikelel iAfrika' fill the air. He was being taken from his family and friends, but in the years ahead he would become the figurehead of the movement fighting for freedom.

An ideal to die for

'During my lifetime I have dedicated myself to this struggle of the African people. I have fought against white domination and I have fought against black domination. I have cherished the ideal of a **democratic** and free society in which all persons live together in harmony and with equal opportunities. It is an ideal which I hope to live for and achieve. But if needs be, it is an ideal for which I am prepared to die.'

(From Mandela's speech, at the Rivonia Trial, 12 July 1964.
From Long Walk to Freedom, 1994)

Robben Island

Nelson Mandela was aged 46 when he returned to Robben Island. The year was 1964, he was prisoner number 466, his cell was about two metres (six feet) wide and he was allowed one visitor every six months. In his tiny damp cell with one window that looked out over a courtyard, Mandela had no radio and newspapers were forbidden. He was restricted to writing and receiving one letter of just 500 words every six months. His bed was a thin mat on the hard floor and he had three thin blankets that barely kept him warm during the winter. There was no running water and he used a bucket rather than a toilet. Years ago he had campaigned against the food at Fort Hare, but now his diet was mainly mealie pap, a kind of porridge made from maize (corn).

▲ *Prisoners crush stones in the prison yard at Robben Island in about 1965. Mandela is probably the fifth from the left in the second row.*

Prison routine

The days slipped into a monotonous routine. His wake-up call was 5.30 a.m. and at 6.45 a.m. he was allowed out of his cell to empty and clean his bucket. After breakfast he worked in a quarry crushing stones to make gravel which was probably used for building roads. Lunch, a drink made from maize and yeast, was served at midday. Then it was more work until 4 p.m. At 4.30 p.m. it was supper, and at 8.30 p.m. everybody was told to sleep. Time seemed to creep by slowly, but he attempted to remain sane by keeping a calendar on the wall of his cell.

The University of Robben Island

During these long days the company of so many other **political prisoners** was a great comfort. Mandela was surrounded by people from different backgrounds and education. After the first few months the authorities allowed the prisoners to study. Some prisoners were **illiterate** so Mandela and some of the other educated prisoners taught them to read and write. Even while they worked in the quarry those with degrees taught their subject to the others. In the evenings Mandela studied towards a law degree through a **correspondence course** with the University of London. Often it was difficult to get the books he needed because these were banned or he couldn't afford them. Gradually he was allowed more books and he studied subjects like **Afrikaner** history and economics as well as law. He also began to write his **autobiography**, but when he was caught he was punished by not being able to study for four years.

During his years at Robben Island, Mandela became a kind of leader to the other prisoners. He helped the younger prisoners, but he also stood up for their rights and organized hunger strikes or go-slows. The freedom fighter who had planned a **terrorist** army also became wiser. 'Strong convictions are the secret of surviving deprivation,' he wrote in his autobiography, 'your spirit can be full even when your stomach is empty.'

▲ *Nelson Mandela talks with his friend Walter Sisulu in the prison yard in 1966. This is one of the few known photographs taken of Mandela during his time in captivity.*

Family matters

Thinking about his family brought Mandela great pain and he often struggled with guilt and regret for what had happened to them. Over the years Winnie had been harassed by the police, **banned** and imprisoned. To add to her troubles she was dismissed from her job as a social worker and often had to rely upon the support of friends. On her rare visits to her husband they were separated by a glass barrier and they had to speak into microphones. Mandela hated not being able to touch his wife and felt frustrated by his inability to help her. Sometimes her visits only lasted half an hour, and in that short time they discussed the progress of their daughters Zeni and Zindzi. Mandela did not see Zindzi until 1975 and he had his first contact visit with Zeni a few years later.

Mandela worried about his children from his first marriage too. In 1968 his mother visited with his daughter Maki and son Makgatho, but his eldest son Thembi refused to either write or visit his father. A few weeks after her visit his mother died, but Mandela was refused permission to attend her funeral. When Thembi died in a car crash in 1969 he wasn't allowed to go to his funeral either. These losses led him to question his past actions: 'Did I make the right decision in leaving my family and letting my children grow up without security?' In the end he believed he would have done it all again, 'In South Africa it is hard for a man to ignore the needs of the people, even at the expense of his family.'

News of the outside world

When Mandela first arrived at Robben Island he wasn't allowed newspapers or magazines. It wasn't until 1980 that he could buy his own daily newspaper. When Winnie visited they were forbidden to discuss any political matters, and so for many years Mandela heard about events in South Africa second-hand through the new prisoners that arrived on the island. The situation for blacks in South Africa continued to get tougher and in the 1960s political activity by blacks had been practically stamped out by the government. By the 1970s a black student called Steve Biko had formed the Black People's Convention, a political group whose aim it was to raise '**Black Consciousness**'. He believed that non-whites should band together and demonstrate against the government for improved conditions for blacks – it was a new voice of hope.

FOR DETAILS ON KEY PEOPLE OF MANDELA'S TIME, SEE PAGES 58-9.

Soweto uprising

In June 1976, 15,000 school children in Soweto marched in protest against overcrowding and bad conditions in their schools. When two children were killed by the police, riots broke out and spread to other **townships**. By the end of 1976, the violence had led to 576 people being killed, 2389 being wounded and thousands of arrests. Mandela's response to this slaughter was smuggled out of prison by another prisoner who was leaving Robben Island. Mandela supported violent opposition: 'Those who live by the gun shall perish by the gun,' he said, 'Unite! Mobilise! Fight On!'

In 1977 Steve Biko was killed while he was in police custody. South Africa seemed to be on the brink of a **revolution** with the terrifying prospect of a war erupting between black and white South Africans. The price of the struggle was high, but Mandela took heart because his people were fighting back: 'The little that filters through these grim walls convinces us that our forces are making progress,' Mandela wrote to a friend in 1978. Meanwhile, after years of protest, the conditions on Robben Island slowly became more tolerable as

▼ *21 June 1976. South African school children rioting in protest against conditions in schools. They were especially angry at being forced to learn in Afrikaans, the language of white Afrikaners.*

the manual labour was finally ended. In his free time Mandela now started a small garden in the prison courtyard. He grew tomatoes, chillies and onions and even gave some of his crop to the prison guards.

Free Mandela

In 1980 the 'Free Mandela' campaign started in Johannesburg and spread across the globe. Mandela became the world's most famous prisoner and the figurehead of the black struggle for equality and justice. He even had pop songs written about him. Marches and anti-**apartheid** demonstrations were held in London and New York, and the **United Nations** called for his release. Ordinary people around the world made their own protest by refusing to buy food or products imported from

South Africa. The South African government would not budge, but conditions on Robben Island did get slightly better. Mandela was allowed to resume his degree after a four-year ban. He could also buy groceries for himself and birthday presents for his children.

◀ *An anti-apartheid demonstration in London in 1984. The banner in the picture demands that South Africa's president, P.W. Botha, free Nelson Mandela.*

9 The end in sight

In March 1982, after eighteen years at Robben Island, Mandela was told to pack up his belongings because he was being transferred, along with Walter Sisulu, Ahmed Kathrada and Raymond Mhlaba, to Pollsmoor prison, just outside Cape Town. At Pollsmoor conditions were much better, and Mandela described their new quarters as 'the prison's **penthouse**' because their room was spacious and they had proper beds and toilets. They had radio and television, more books to read, and even the food was better. Mandela appreciated the changes but he hated the wrench from his friends at Robben Island and missed his garden. Soon he started a new garden, and in 1984 he had his first 'contact' visit from Winnie: 'I kissed and held my wife for the first time in all these many years. It was a moment I had dreamed about a thousand times.'

Violence and vehemence

While life was more comfortable for Mandela, the situation in South Africa continued to worsen. High unemployment and rising prices badly affected the poorest people, and these were mostly black. This made anger against white people even greater and violent **rebellions** in the **townships** became part of South African life. An ANC car bomb that exploded in Pretoria, killing nineteen people and injuring over 200 others, sent shock waves through the white community. In the same year 700 anti-**apartheid** organizations, many of which were white, formed the United **Democratic** Front (UDF). President P.W. Botha relaxed some apartheid laws, such as the **pass laws**, and invested more money in black education. It was an attempt to appease the black community, but people wanted more – they wanted an end to all apartheid and they wanted the vote.

▲ *School students in 1986 protest against apartheid in Soweto during the state of emergency. Mandela once said that life in prison was nothing compared to the suffering of his people outside jail.*

In prison Mandela was granted more visitors and they told him about the unstable situation in the country. He was saddened by the loss of life and frustrated that he could do nothing to help. By now he accepted that white people were part of South Africa. 'We want them to live here with us and share power with us,' he told an American journalist. Meanwhile the international community increased pressure on the government to release Mandela and abandon apartheid. In 1986 the USA and many European countries imposed **sanctions** and withdrew business from South Africa. They hoped that by attacking the economic prosperity of the whites the South African government would be forced to abandon apartheid. Sporting links to South Africa were also cut and many entertainers refused to work there. South Africa's government had fewer and fewer friends in the world, and the release of Mandela became a crucial issue in South Africa.

▲ President P. W. Botha was known as the 'Great Crocodile' because of his ferocious temper. After their first meeting Mandela described him as courteous and friendly and believed he was a man with whom he could negotiate for change.

In 1985 Botha offered freedom to Mandela and other political prisoners in return for their rejection of violence. Mandela's response was delivered by his daughter Zindzi at a stadium in Soweto. It was the first time Mandela's own words had been heard in public for two decades, and he stood firm: 'I cherish my own freedom, but I care even more for your freedom. I will not give any undertaking when you and I, the people, are not free.'

Freedom talks

During the 1980s there was a rise in violence between different groups of blacks who disagreed over how the future black South African government would be formed. Most of this violence took place in the townships which, at times, became almost ungovernable. In July 1985 the government declared a **state of emergency** in South Africa. The situation had become so frightening that Mandela decided to talk with the government. In 1986 the first of the secret **negotiations** for his release began. Around the world his image had become larger than life. A statue of him had been unveiled in London and in July 1988 a concert in London entitled 'Freedom at 70' was watched by 200 million television viewers from around the world. Shortly after his 70th birthday Mandela developed **tuberculosis** – years of living in damp cells had taken their toll. The government panicked – what would happen if Mandela died in prison? There would almost certainly be more violence. They knew that they needed to reach a solution as quickly as possible.

Victor Verster prison

Mandela pulled through his illness and in December 1988 he was transferred to Victor Verster prison which was 35 miles from Cape Town. This time he had his own bungalow in the grounds of the prison. There were guest bedrooms and bathrooms, a kitchen with all modern conveniences and even a cook to prepare his favourite meals. Mandela was certain this was a sign that he was going to be released, but he was determined that his freedom would be on his terms. He wanted to talk to President Botha and explain that he, Mandela, was not part of the problem but part of the solution. The following January Botha suffered a stroke but the two finally met in July 1989. By now presidential elections in South Africa were set for September. Following the vote, Mandela would be up against a new National Party leader, President F. W. de Klerk.

Respecting other people's point of view

'Something that Nelson and Walter taught me, personally, was the whole question of respecting other people for their point of view, even if you disagreed with it.'

(Neville Alexander, taken from *Robben Island: Our University*, 1988)

10 Free at last

FOR DETAILS ON KEY PEOPLE OF MANDELA'S TIME, SEE PAGES 58-9.

In October 1989 de Klerk announced that Walter Sisulu, Ahmed Kathrada, Raymond Mhlaba and other fellow prisoners would be freed. A few days later Mandela said goodbye to his friends. In December he donned a suit and met de Klerk for the first time. Mandela genuinely respected the president who listened to his demands and though de Klerk made no promises, Mandela recognized he 'was a man we could do business with'. On 2 February 1990 de Klerk opened parliament with a groundbreaking speech that showed his determination to dismantle **apartheid**. He removed the ban on the ANC and other anti-apartheid organizations. Mandela described it as 'a breathtaking moment, for in one sweeping action he had virtually normalized the situation in South Africa'. Seven days later de Klerk and Mandela met once more. The following day Mandela was at last released.

▼ *The magical moment when Nelson Mandela walked free from Victor Verster Prison on 11 February 1990.*

The day of freedom

On the day he was freed from prison Mandela awoke at 4.30 a.m., he exercised, washed and then ate breakfast just as he usually did. But 11 February 1990 was a day like no other. That afternoon, after 10,000 days in prison, he would be a free man. After breakfast Mandela worked on his speech then he began packing his belongings. After all these years his possessions, mainly books, filled just over a dozen boxes. Winnie, Walter Sisulu and other friends and family arrived shortly after 2 p.m. and just before 4 p.m. he was driven to the front gate of the prison. Mandela and Winnie got out of the car and walked hand-in-hand to the gate. Ahead of them was a huge crowd of journalists and well-wishers. Cameras flashed and reporters pushed microphones towards him. Before he knew it Mandela was swallowed up by the crowd. Mandela raised his right fist, a victory salute for the ANC, and a massive roar of applause filled the air. After 27 years he was free and his people were rejoicing. It was an emotional moment and around the world many people turned on their televisions and radios to capture its magic. Minutes later Mandela stepped back into the car and made his way to City Hall in Cape Town where he made his first speech as a free man.

March to freedom

'Our march to freedom is irreversible. We must not allow fears to stand in our way. Universal **suffrage** *on a common voters' roll in a united,* **democratic** *and non-racial South Africa is the only way to peace and racial harmony.'*

(Excerpt from Mandela's speech on the day of his release)

Just an ordinary man

It had been a long walk to freedom but now he had another hard road ahead – freedom and **democracy** for his people. At the age of 71 Mandela re-entered the ANC. Many people believed he could bring about a better future for South Africa, but could he live up to people's expectations? At his first ANC meetings Mandela listened more than he spoke. He realized that if the ANC were to govern the country then they needed to think carefully about their strategy. They were no longer a party fighting for freedom, now they needed to be taken seriously as politicians who would one day govern the country.

Ambassador for South Africa

For the next six months Mandela travelled extensively promoting and raising funds for the ANC and urging countries to maintain their economic **sanctions** until the South African government had abolished apartheid. First of all he visited African countries like Zambia, Namibia and Zimbabwe; then he travelled to Europe, the USA and Asia. Everywhere he went he was received with respect and affection and treated like the president of South Africa. In April 1990 he was in London where he attended a concert held in his honour. At the end he strode onto the stage and told the crowd, 'You elected not to forget. Even through the thickness of the prison walls…we heard your voices demanding our freedom.' In June he was in Harlem, New York, where once again he showed his amazing ability for forgiveness and his vision of peace, 'Death to racism!' he said, 'Glory to the sisterhood and brotherhood of peoples throughout the world!' In October he was in Delhi, the capital of India, where he thanked India for sending the world Gandhi – the originator of non-violent protest.

▶ *Four months after his release Mandela visited Harlem, a poor black neighbourhood of New York in the USA. Crowds of well-wishers cheered and waved photographs of him.*

President of the ANC

In June 1991, at the first national conference of the ANC held within South Africa since its ban, Mandela was elected president of the ANC. As president he showed that there was no time for bitterness. With his sweet smile and wonderful sense of humour it was a surprise to find he also had a hard side. This steely backbone saw him through the difficult days ahead. In December 1991 he began his first talks with President de Klerk about the future of South Africa. At the Convention for a Democratic South Africa (Codesa) they negotiated over how South Africa would be governed. Mandela wanted majority rule by one party. De Klerk did not want majority rule as he feared the ANC would win the election and this would lead to black majority rule. At times their **negotiations** became heated, but Mandela continued to pressure the president to make reforms to the South African government.

▲ Armed fighting between supporters of the Inkatha Freedom Party and the ANC turned South Africa into a killing-ground in the years running up to the 1994 elections. Mandela pleaded with South Africans to 'End this war now!'

Difficult days

Behind the public face Mandela's own private life was in turmoil. His eldest daughter Maki told him, 'You are a father to all our people, but you have never had the time to be a father to me.' It was painful being reminded of his failures. His relationship with Winnie was also causing him much sorrow. They had moved from his old house in Orlando into a larger house that Winnie had specially built for them in Soweto. Mandela was uncomfortable with the grandeur of the house. There were also rumours that Winnie had been involved in the kidnapping and murder of a black youth, Stompie Seipei (in 1991 she was convicted of Stompie's kidnapping, but the sentence was reduced on appeal). Though Mandela loved his wife he had to accept that their marriage had not worked out.

In April 1992 he announced their separation. As he told the media his sad news his old friends Oliver Tambo and Walter Sisulu were at his side. A year later Tambo died from a stroke. Mandela was bereft: 'I kept up a life-long conversation with him in my head,' he said.

11 Creating a new South Africa

While Mandela and de Klerk talked, the violence and loss of life in South Africa increased. Mandela lost faith in de Klerk and the two men battled over the negotiating table for two years until they finally agreed upon majority rule in South Africa. As a compromise, however, there would be a transitional period whereby power would be shared for five years between the winning parties. The date for the first all-race, one-person-one vote election for South Africa was finally set for April 1994. In December of 1993 Mandela and de Klerk travelled to Oslo in Norway to accept a joint **Nobel Peace Prize** for their part in negotiating a **democratic** South Africa. In January 1994 Mandela launched his presidential campaign. The new Nelson Mandela, often appearing in bright-coloured shirts with jazzy designs, took time to talk to people in the crowds, especially children. On one occasion a child asked him why he wore such bright shirts. 'You must remember,' Mandela replied, 'I was in jail for twenty-seven years, I want to *feel* freedom.'

▼ *Nelson Mandela and F. W. de Klerk accept a joint Nobel Peace Prize in 1993. 'To make peace with an enemy, one must work with that enemy, and that enemy becomes your partner,' Mandela later wrote.*

Victory for the ANC

At the end of April 1994 it was announced that the ANC had won 62.6 per cent of the vote. At the ANC victory celebration in Johannesburg Mandela told the audience, 'This is a time to heal the old wounds and build a new South Africa.' On 10 May Mandela became the new president, with de Klerk and Thabo Mbeki (now the current president of South Africa) as deputy presidents. In his **inauguration** speech Mandela went back to the themes of freedom, **reconciliation** and peace. Afterwards the South African airforce did a fly-by and helicopters trailed the new South African flag. The crowd also joined together to sing the two national anthems, 'Die Stem', the anthem of old South Africa, and the ANC's 'Nkosi Sikelel iAfrika' (God bless Africa).

South Africa's new flag

This new flag was adopted in 1994 and represents the coming together of all the peoples of South Africa.

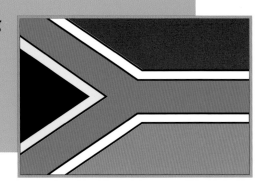

A rainbow nation

Nelson Mandela served just one term (five years) as president but in that time he brought hope to South Africa. To help heal the wounds of years of racial division he formed his government from people of different races, religions and political persuasions – democracy had at last come to all the people of the 'rainbow nation'. He took over the president's offices in Pretoria and Cape Town and moved into the Groote Schuur estate, the grand mansion residence of previous South

▲ *President Mandela stands beside his daughter Zenani at his presidential inauguration in May 1994.*

African presidents. He changed very little in these places and even kept on many of the staff, including **Afrikaners**, who had worked for previous governments.

Mandela often surprised people with his good grace and gentlemanly behaviour. He took time to talk and listen to ordinary people and made a special effort to make white South Africans feel comfortable and included in the new South Africa. Symbolic gestures like appearing in a Springbok (the South African all-white rugby team) rugby shirt at the World Cup Final earned him the love and respect of many white South Africans. Mandela believed in leading by example, and within three months of taking office, his country had become a more peaceful place. The introduction of the Reconstruction and Development Programme, which promised to build new low-cost housing, improve health and education, and redistribute 30 per cent of the land in South Africa, added to the new climate of optimism.

▶ *President Mandela won the hearts of many white South Africans when he awarded the Springboks with the cup in the Rugby World Cup in 1995. Mandela always believed that sport was a way of uniting all South Africans.*

Public versus private man

Once more Mandela acted as ambassador for South Africa and played host to some of the most famous people in the world. Princess Diana and Prince Charles of Britain, President Bill Clinton of the USA and Fidel Castro, the **communist** leader of Cuba, paid visits and formed lasting friendships. Visits from pop-stars like the Spice Girls and Michael Jackson were chances to show off the broad Mandela smile and his exceptional sense of humour. But life at the top had its downsides. 'The sad thing is that nobody realizes that my father is very lonely,' said his daughter Zindzi. When Mandela wasn't in his presidential residences he retreated to the new home he had built near his childhood home of Qunu in the Transkei. This simple red-brick house was like the bungalow he lived in at Victor Verster prison. It had no stairs to trouble his legs and had views over the green fields of the Transkei to remind him of his childhood.

In 1995 Mandela announced he was divorcing Winnie, and soon afterwards he was seen in public with Graca Machel, the widow of the former president of Mozambique, Samora Machel. Mandela had first met Graca in 1990 on a visit to Mozambique. She was twenty-eight years younger than him but they shared a humble background and a love of children. Over the years their friendship turned into love and by 1997 Graca was accompanying Mandela on official tours – at last Mandela seemed happier and more carefree. On his eightieth birthday in July 1998 they were married in their home in the Transkei.

12 The legacy of Nelson Mandela

In 1999 Mandela stood down as president. Many people were disappointed that more homes hadn't been built and the conditions for so many poorer black people had hardly improved. The economy had suffered and, sadly, crime figures and violence increased again. In his final speech in parliament Mandela urged his people to be patient, telling them that these changes would take time. Mandela remained a popular figure however, both at home and abroad, and people feared for the future of South Africa now that Mandela was no longer president. To many it seemed that Mandela was the only person who was capable of uniting his country. Though people were sad to see him leave public life they were pleased that he could finally devote time to his own happiness. In his home in the Transkei Mandela would at last have time to enjoy the love and companionship of his wife and the visits from his family, as well as his beautiful garden and his other pleasures, music and reading.

▼ *President Mandela offers his seat in parliament to the new President-elect, Thabo Mbeki, in June 1999.*

The future

In 1999 South Africa's second black president, Thabo Mbeki, had the almost impossible job of following in Mandela's footsteps. Mbeki is younger than Mandela and was educated at university in England. Many people say he is more reserved than his **predecessor**, but many believe he has the necessary strength to lead his country. He faces many challenges as unemployment and poverty within black communities are still very high, and many black people still live in poor quality housing. Rape and murder rates in South Africa are among the highest in the world. Years of violence and unrest have also had a bad effect on the country's economy. Sadly, the South African economy has also been affected by one of the worst AIDS epidemics in the world.

▲ Schoolgirls in South Africa after apartheid had ended. Now Nelson Mandela can be proud of a nation where children of all races attend the same schools and learn about how to build a new South Africa together.

Mandela warned his country that years of neglect could not be reversed overnight, but he gave his people belief in themselves and the courage to tackle the problems ahead. It was his **negotiations** with President de Klerk that ensured that each and every person in South Africa could vote in **democratic** elections. Without Nelson Mandela who is to say whether this would have happened?

In his speeches Mandela always remembered the many others who joined him in the struggle. But it was Mandela's wisdom and strength of character and his ability to forgive that helped bring an end to **apartheid** in South Africa. Nelson Mandela will always be remembered as a man who stood up and faced the enemy with courage, dignity and charm.

Mandela remembered

'I would like to be remembered as part of a team, and I would like my contribution to be assessed as somebody who carried out decisions taken by that collective.'

(Nelson Mandela)

'In his retirement, Nelson Mandela will be the father of the nation. He will continue his role reconciling conflict within South Africa, Africa and internationally.'

(Indres Naidoo, a prisoner on Robben Island, later a government minister)

*'What characterizes his presidency is his human touch and sensitivity toward the disadvantaged and not in a racial way. He is as sensitive to a white child with leukaemia as he is to a **township** child who has been raped, or whose sibling has been murdered.'*

(Jay Naidoo, Minister of Posts, Telecommunications and Broadcasting)

Timeline

1918	July: Rolihlahla Mandela is born in the village of Mvezo, in the Transkei, South Africa.
1927	Mandela's father Chief Gadla Henry Mphakanyiswa dies, and Mandela moves to the 'Great Palace' to live with his uncle Chief Jongintaba Dalindyebo.
1938	Mandela attends Fort Hare University College.
1941	Mandela flees from Transkei to Johannesburg where he meets Walter Sisulu, starts work as a legal clerk and studies at University of Witwatersrand.
1944	Mandela is one of the founders of the African National Congress Youth League.
1944	Marries first wife Evelyn Mase.
1945	Madiba Thembekile Mandela (called Thembi), son, born.
1947	Makaziwe Mandela, daughter, born, dies nine months later.
1950	Mandela joins ANC National Executive. Makgatho Lewanika Mandela, second son, born.
1952	Mandela and Oliver Tambo establish the law firm 'Mandela and Tambo', the first black legal firm in South Africa. Campaign for the Defiance of Unjust Laws is launched.
1952	Mandela is elected as president of the Transvaal branch of the ANC and deputy president of the ANC.
1952	December: First, six month banning order.
1953	Makaziwe Mandela, second daughter (named after the first daughter) born.
1955	Helps to organize Congress of the People, consulted on the Freedom Charter.
1956	December: Mandela and 155 others are arrested for treason. The Treason Trial lasts until 1961. Mandela and Evelyn separate.
1957	Meets Nomzamo Winifred Madikizela.
1958	Mandela divorces Evelyn and marries Winnie.
1959	Zenani Mandela, third daughter, is born.
1960	The ANC is banned. Zindziswa Mandela, fourth daughter, is born.
1961	December: Launch of Umkhonto we Sizwe (MK), Mandela goes underground.
1962	January: Mandela travels throughout Africa, attends conference in Ethiopia, visits Egypt, Nigeria, Ghana and the UK, completes two months' military training

	in Algeria and Ethiopia.
	August: Mandela is arrested and sent to prison on Robben Island.
1963	July: Lilliesleaf farm in Rivonia is raided by the police. Mandela is charged with sabotage in the Rivonia Trial.
1964	June: Mandela is sentenced to life imprisonment in maximum security prison, Robben Island.
1968	Mandela's mother Nosekeni Fanny dies.
1969	Thembi Mandela is killed in a car crash.
1982	April: Mandela is moved from Robben Island to Pollsmoor Prison in Cape Town.
1984	Winnie is allowed the first contact visit to her husband in over 21 years.
1985	President P.W. Botha says he will release Mandela if he rejects violence – Mandela says the government must reject violence first.
1986	Begins secret talks with the South African government.
1988	Mandela suffers from tuberculosis, moves into private bungalow in the grounds of Victor Verster Prison.
1990	February: Mandela is freed after 10,000 days in prison, returns to Soweto two days later.
1991	June: Mandela is elected president of the ANC when Oliver Tambo steps down through ill health.
	December: Convention for a Democratic South Africa (CODESA) begins.
1992	April: Mandela announces separation from Winnie.
1993	Mandela and de Klerk are awarded the Nobel Peace Prize.
1994	April: Mandela casts his first vote in the presidential elections.
	May: Mandela becomes the president of South Africa.
1997	December: Mandela steps down as ANC president.
1998	July: Mandela marries Graca Machel on his eightieth birthday, they tour the world saying goodbye to world leaders.
1999	February: President Mandela's final opening of parliament.
	March: President Mandela hands over to the new president, Thabo Mbeki.
	June: Mandela retires from public life.

Key people of Mandela's time

Oliver Tambo (1917–93). President of the ANC from 1967 until 1990. Like Mandela he was born in the Transkei and attended Fort Hare University College. He met Mandela again in Johannesburg in the early 1940s and they became life-long friends. When the ANC was banned in 1960 he left South Africa for Tanganyika (Tanzania) and London where he set up external wings of the ANC. Tambo travelled extensively raising support for action against the South African government. After three decades in exile, Tambo returned to South Africa in 1991. In July 1991, at the ANC's first national conference in South Africa, he was elected National Chairperson of the ANC. He died from a stroke in April 1993.

Walter Sisulu (1912–). As one of the Rivonia eight, Sisulu was sentenced to life imprisonment in 1964. In 1949 he became Secretary General of the ANC. Following a banning order he resigned his post in 1959, but continued to work **underground**. During his years in prison on Robben Island he studied for a BA degree in art history and anthropology. He was released from prison in October 1989 and at the ANC's first national conference in South Africa, in July 1991, he was elected deputy president of the ANC.

Winnie Nomzamo Madikizela (1934–). Second wife of Nelson Mandela until their divorce in 1996. In 1958 she was held in detention for her part in a demonstration against **pass laws**. While Mandela was in prison (1964-1990) she continued to campaign for black rights and for her husband's release. From 1969 to 1970 she was **banned** and imprisoned, before finally being banned from Johannesburg from 1977 to 1985. Upon her return to Soweto in 1985 she became more militant and outspoken. Allegations of her involvement in the kidnapping and murder of a black youth in Soweto brought her increasing unpopularity. In 1997 she was re-elected the president of the ANC Woman's League.

Frederik Willem de Klerk (1936–). Last South African president (1989-1994) elected under the **apartheid** system. He was appointed vice president in Nelson Mandela's coalition government in 1994. De Klerk began his career in law before becoming an MP in 1972. He later served on the cabinet of presidents John Vorster and P.W. Botha where he backed policies such as preventing blacks from entering white universities. He replaced P.W. Botha as president in 1989. In February 1990 he ended the 30-year ban on the ANC. His **negotiations** with Mandela ended white minority rule in South Africa. In 1993 he shared the **Nobel Peace Prize** with Mandela. He resigned from politics in 1997.

Steven Biko (1946–77). South African black activist who became politically active while studying medicine at Natal University. He became president of the newly founded South African Students Organization (SASO) in 1969. He spoke out against **white supremacy** and, with his supporters, set up the Black Communities Project which went on to develop self-help schemes. In 1971 he founded the Black People's Convention, an organization that promoted '**Black Consciousness**'. He was detained by the police four times before he died in police custody following a brutal beating in September 1977.

Further reading

Further reading

Freedom Song, the story of Nelson Mandela, Neil Tonge and
Tony Morris, Hodder Wayland, 2002

11 February 1990: The Release of Nelson Mandela, John Malam,
Cherrytree Books, 2002

The Story of Nelson Mandela, James Riordan and Neil Reed,
Belitha Press, 2001

Profiles: Nelson Mandela, Sean Connolly, Heinemann Library, 2001

Websites

The official site for the African National Congress (ANC) which
includes profiles and biographical notes about its major
members, including the former president of South Africa,
Nelson Mandela
http://www.anc.org.za/people/mandela.html

A brief overview of Mandela's life and political career
http://www.facts.com/cd/b94314.htm

An interview with Mandela in February 2000, the tenth
anniversary of his release from Robben Island
http://www.csmonitor.com/durable/2000/02/10/p15s1.htm

Sources

Key History for GCSE: South Africa, Hamish MacDonald and Barry
Williamson, Stanley Thornes, 1997

Mandela, Charlene Smith, Johnnic, 1999

Long Walk to Freedom, Nelson Mandela, Abacus, 1994

Mandela: The Authorized Biography, Anthony Sampson, Harper
Collins, 1999

The Lady: The Life and Times of Winnie Mandela, Emma Gilbey,
Jonathan Cape, 1993

The Mammoth Book of How It Happened edited by Jon E. Lewis,
Robinson, 1998

A History of South Africa, Martin Roberts, Longman, 1990

Glossary

Afrikaners white South Africans who were descended from the Dutch colonists who came to South Africa in the seventeenth century

apartheid policy in South Africa of keeping people of different races apart

attorney person, usually a lawyer, who acts for another party or person in legal matters

autobiography story or book written by a person about their life

bail sum of money that is paid to a court which allows the person charged of a crime to remain free until their trial in court

ballot piece of paper that is used for making a vote

banned under apartheid in South Africa a banned person was not allowed to attend meetings of more than one person at a time, appear in public, have their speeches mentioned in the media or leave the country. If they broke the ban they could be punished by imprisonment.

Black Consciousness being aware, and proud of one's identity as a black person

boycott organized protest where a group of people refuse to have dealings with a person or an organization for example by refusing to buy products from a shop or use public transport

charter written description of an organization's functions and ideas

civil rights the rights of individuals to equality and justice

civil servant person employed by the state or government of a country to deal with civil affairs such as taxation

civil war war between different groups of people within one country. An inter-racial civil war would be between people of different racial backgrounds.

colonial a system whereby a land and its people are ruled from another country

communism way of organizing a country so that the land, its housing and its industries belong to the state, and the profits are shared between everybody. A communist is someone who supports this system.

congress another word for a formal meeting of people

correspondence course study of a course or degree by post

democratic describes a system where the government is elected by its people, and is therefore accountable to them

eloquent to use language effectively and speak well

eviction act of removing people from a property by legal means

expulsion act of expelling or throwing a person out of a place or an organization

fugitive person who runs away or hides from an enemy or escapes the law

guerrilla warfare a form of warfare conducted by small numbers of irregular troops rather than by large standing armies

illiterate not able to read or write

inauguration ceremony admitting a new president to office

incriminating making someone appear guilty of a crime

Law Society official organization that regulates solicitors and lawyers

liberation act of setting somebody or something free from an enemy or oppressive society

mass demonstrations organized protests by a large group of people such as strikes or boycotts

maximum security prison prison with extra security where people who are considered a big risk to the general public are imprisoned

Methodist member of the Christian Protestant church founded by John and Charles Wesley in England in the eighteenth century

missionaries people who are sent to a foreign country usually to educate and convert people to their religion

negotiation act of talking about something so an agreement can be made between people or organizations with different views

Nobel Peace Prize award given each year to the person or organization that has made the greatest contribution to world peace

passbook an official document which all non-white South Africans had to carry at all times during apartheid. No black person was allowed to remain in a white area for longer than 72 hours unless they had special permission

pass laws laws that restricted the movements of blacks within South Africa

penthouse home or apartment on the top floor of a building. As this apartment was often considered to be the best in the block the penthouse is now associated with being the best accommodation.

political prisoner someone who is imprisoned for their political beliefs

predecessor person who formerly held a post or position of power

raid surprise attack or search of one's home by the police

ramshackle old and untidy appearance – often used to describe poor housing

rebellion openly resisting authority, sometimes violently

reconciliation being friendly with somebody who was once an enemy

recruiting attracting or gathering new followers to a group

republic country that is not ruled by a monarch but that has an elected head of state

reviled criticized and talked about in an abusive manner

revolution rebellion to overthrow the government

sabotage deliberate destruction of equipment and machinery to weaken an enemy

sanctions actions or measures taken against a country by other countries in order to force a change of policy. From the 1970s many countries had sanctions that boycotted South African goods.

segregated separation of different racial groups

state of emergency period of time in which the government of a country employs the army, and arrests political opponents, in order to remain in power

stay-at-home type of organized political protest in which masses of people do not go to work, use public services or attend shops for a set period of time

strike refuse to work

suffrage the right to vote in political elections

terrorist person who uses or favours the use of violence to bring about political change

township small town or an area of a South African town or city that has been set aside for black housing

trade union an organisation set up to promote better wages and conditions for workers

treason crime against the government or ruler of a country

tuberculosis infectious disease of the lungs

underground describes the hidden or secret activities of a political group that aims to topple the existing government

United Nations an international organization of governments of independent states. The United Nations was set up in 1945 to promote peace and understanding between nations of the world.

violation disobeying or failing to comply with a law

white supremacy theory that white people are superior to people of other races

Xhosa large black ethnic group of people who live mainly in the eastern Cape province

Index